THIS ADDRESS BOOK BELONGS TO:

_____

>>>————<<<

Dear Customer,

Thank you so much for choosing a Creative Media Press (CMP) address book.

If you enjoyed using our address book then please support us and leave a review.

Best wishes,

The Creative Media Press Team

Other books sold on Amazon by CMP you might enjoy:

- CMP Address Books
- CMP Reading Logs and Journals
- CMP Gratitude Journals
- CMP Notebooks

You can also find CMP Books on Facebook.

Creative Media Press Ltd
71-75 Shelton Street
Covent Garden
London
WC2H 9JQ

Copyright © Creative Media Press Ltd

All rights reserved. No part of this work may be reproduced, or utiliized in any form
or by any means, electronic or mechanical, including photocopying, recording
or by any information storage and retrieval system, without the prior written permission of the publisher.

CMP

A

NAME:

ADDRESS:

PHONE:

EMAIL:

BIRTHDAY:

>>———<<

NAME:

ADDRESS:

PHONE:

EMAIL:

BIRTHDAY:

>>———<<

NAME:

ADDRESS:

PHONE:

EMAIL:

BIRTHDAY:

A

NAME:

ADDRESS:

PHONE:

EMAIL:

BIRTHDAY:

>>> ———— <<<

NAME:

ADDRESS:

PHONE:

EMAIL:

BIRTHDAY:

>>> ———— <<<

NAME:

ADDRESS:

PHONE:

EMAIL:

BIRTHDAY:

A

NAME:

ADDRESS:

PHONE:

EMAIL:

BIRTHDAY:

>>>————<<<

NAME:

ADDRESS:

PHONE:

EMAIL:

BIRTHDAY:

>>>————<<<

NAME:

ADDRESS:

PHONE:

EMAIL:

BIRTHDAY:

A

NAME:

ADDRESS:

PHONE:

EMAIL:

BIRTHDAY:

NAME:

ADDRESS:

PHONE:

EMAIL:

BIRTHDAY:

NAME:

ADDRESS:

PHONE:

EMAIL:

BIRTHDAY:

B

NAME:

ADDRESS:

PHONE:

EMAIL:

BIRTHDAY:

>>———<<

NAME:

ADDRESS:

PHONE:

EMAIL:

BIRTHDAY:

>>———<<

NAME:

ADDRESS:

PHONE:

EMAIL:

BIRTHDAY:

B

NAME:

ADDRESS:

PHONE:

EMAIL:

BIRTHDAY:

NAME:

ADDRESS:

PHONE:

EMAIL:

BIRTHDAY:

NAME:

ADDRESS:

PHONE:

EMAIL:

BIRTHDAY:

NAME:

ADDRESS:

PHONE:

EMAIL:

BIRTHDAY:

B

>>> ———— <<<

NAME:

ADDRESS:

PHONE:

EMAIL:

BIRTHDAY:

>>> ———— <<<

NAME:

ADDRESS:

PHONE:

EMAIL:

BIRTHDAY:

B

NAME:

ADDRESS:

PHONE:

EMAIL:

BIRTHDAY:

>>>———<<<

NAME:

ADDRESS:

PHONE:

EMAIL:

BIRTHDAY:

>>>———<<<

NAME:

ADDRESS:

PHONE:

EMAIL:

BIRTHDAY:

C

NAME:

ADDRESS:

PHONE:

EMAIL:

BIRTHDAY:

>>>———<<<

NAME:

ADDRESS:

PHONE:

EMAIL:

BIRTHDAY:

>>>———<<<

NAME:

ADDRESS:

PHONE:

EMAIL:

BIRTHDAY:

C

NAME:

ADDRESS:

PHONE:

EMAIL:

BIRTHDAY:

NAME:

ADDRESS:

PHONE:

EMAIL:

BIRTHDAY:

NAME:

ADDRESS:

PHONE:

EMAIL:

BIRTHDAY:

C

NAME:

ADDRESS:

PHONE:

EMAIL:

BIRTHDAY:

>>———<<

NAME:

ADDRESS:

PHONE:

EMAIL:

BIRTHDAY:

>>———<<

NAME:

ADDRESS:

PHONE:

EMAIL:

BIRTHDAY:

C

NAME:

ADDRESS:

PHONE:

EMAIL:

BIRTHDAY:

>>>———<<<

NAME:

ADDRESS:

PHONE:

EMAIL:

BIRTHDAY:

>>>———<<<

NAME:

ADDRESS:

PHONE:

EMAIL:

BIRTHDAY:

D

NAME:

ADDRESS:

PHONE:

EMAIL:

BIRTHDAY:

>>>———<<<

NAME:

ADDRESS:

PHONE:

EMAIL:

BIRTHDAY:

>>>———<<<

NAME:

ADDRESS:

PHONE:

EMAIL:

BIRTHDAY:

D

NAME:

ADDRESS:

PHONE:

EMAIL:

BIRTHDAY:

>>>————<<<

NAME:

ADDRESS:

PHONE:

EMAIL:

BIRTHDAY:

>>>————<<<

NAME:

ADDRESS:

PHONE:

EMAIL:

BIRTHDAY:

D

NAME:

ADDRESS:

PHONE:

EMAIL:

BIRTHDAY:

>>———<<

NAME:

ADDRESS:

PHONE:

EMAIL:

BIRTHDAY:

>>———<<

NAME:

ADDRESS:

PHONE:

EMAIL:

BIRTHDAY:

D

NAME:

ADDRESS:

PHONE:

EMAIL:

BIRTHDAY:

>>>———<<<

NAME:

ADDRESS:

PHONE:

EMAIL:

BIRTHDAY:

>>>———<<<

NAME:

ADDRESS:

PHONE:

EMAIL:

BIRTHDAY:

E

NAME:

ADDRESS:

PHONE:

EMAIL:

BIRTHDAY:

>>>———<<<

NAME:

ADDRESS:

PHONE:

EMAIL:

BIRTHDAY:

>>>———<<<

NAME:

ADDRESS:

PHONE:

EMAIL:

BIRTHDAY:

E

NAME:

ADDRESS:

PHONE:

EMAIL:

BIRTHDAY:

>>> ———— <<<

NAME:

ADDRESS:

PHONE:

EMAIL:

BIRTHDAY:

>>> ———— <<<

NAME:

ADDRESS:

PHONE:

EMAIL:

BIRTHDAY:

E

NAME:

ADDRESS:

PHONE:

EMAIL:

BIRTHDAY:

>>———<<

NAME:

ADDRESS:

PHONE:

EMAIL:

BIRTHDAY:

>>———<<

NAME:

ADDRESS:

PHONE:

EMAIL:

BIRTHDAY:

E

NAME:

ADDRESS:

PHONE:

EMAIL:

BIRTHDAY:

>>> ———— <<<

NAME:

ADDRESS:

PHONE:

EMAIL:

BIRTHDAY:

>>> ———— <<<

NAME:

ADDRESS:

PHONE:

EMAIL:

BIRTHDAY:

F

NAME:

ADDRESS:

PHONE:

EMAIL:

BIRTHDAY:

>>>———<<<

NAME:

ADDRESS:

PHONE:

EMAIL:

BIRTHDAY:

>>>———<<<

NAME:

ADDRESS:

PHONE:

EMAIL:

BIRTHDAY:

F

NAME:

ADDRESS:

PHONE:

EMAIL:

BIRTHDAY:

>>> ———— <<<

NAME:

ADDRESS:

PHONE:

EMAIL:

BIRTHDAY:

>>> ———— <<<

NAME:

ADDRESS:

PHONE:

EMAIL:

BIRTHDAY:

F

NAME:

ADDRESS:

PHONE:

EMAIL:

BIRTHDAY:

>>>———<<<

NAME:

ADDRESS:

PHONE:

EMAIL:

BIRTHDAY:

>>>———<<<

NAME:

ADDRESS:

PHONE:

EMAIL:

BIRTHDAY:

F

NAME:

ADDRESS:

PHONE:

EMAIL:

BIRTHDAY:

>>> ———— <<<

NAME:

ADDRESS:

PHONE:

EMAIL:

BIRTHDAY:

>>> ———— <<<

NAME:

ADDRESS:

PHONE:

EMAIL:

BIRTHDAY:

G

NAME:

ADDRESS:

PHONE:

EMAIL:

BIRTHDAY:

>>>———<<<

NAME:

ADDRESS:

PHONE:

EMAIL:

BIRTHDAY:

>>>———<<<

NAME:

ADDRESS:

PHONE:

EMAIL:

BIRTHDAY:

G

NAME:

ADDRESS:

PHONE:

EMAIL:

BIRTHDAY:

>>> ———— <<<

NAME:

ADDRESS:

PHONE:

EMAIL:

BIRTHDAY:

>>> ———— <<<

NAME:

ADDRESS:

PHONE:

EMAIL:

BIRTHDAY:

G

NAME:

ADDRESS:

PHONE:

EMAIL:

BIRTHDAY:

>>———<<

NAME:

ADDRESS:

PHONE:

EMAIL:

BIRTHDAY:

>>———<<

NAME:

ADDRESS:

PHONE:

EMAIL:

BIRTHDAY:

G

NAME:

ADDRESS:

PHONE:

EMAIL:

BIRTHDAY:

>>>———<<<

NAME:

ADDRESS:

PHONE:

EMAIL:

BIRTHDAY:

>>>———<<<

NAME:

ADDRESS:

PHONE:

EMAIL:

BIRTHDAY:

NAME:
ADDRESS:

PHONE:
EMAIL:
BIRTHDAY:

>>> ———— <<<

NAME:
ADDRESS:

PHONE:
EMAIL:
BIRTHDAY:

>>> ———— <<<

NAME:
ADDRESS:

PHONE:
EMAIL:
BIRTHDAY:

H

NAME:

ADDRESS:

PHONE:

EMAIL:

BIRTHDAY:

>>>————<<<

NAME:

ADDRESS:

PHONE:

EMAIL:

BIRTHDAY:

>>>————<<<

NAME:

ADDRESS:

PHONE:

EMAIL:

BIRTHDAY:

H

NAME:

ADDRESS:

PHONE:

EMAIL:

BIRTHDAY:

NAME:

ADDRESS:

PHONE:

EMAIL:

BIRTHDAY:

NAME:

ADDRESS:

PHONE:

EMAIL:

BIRTHDAY:

H

NAME:

ADDRESS:

PHONE:

EMAIL:

BIRTHDAY:

NAME:

ADDRESS:

PHONE:

EMAIL:

BIRTHDAY:

NAME:

ADDRESS:

PHONE:

EMAIL:

BIRTHDAY:

NAME:

ADDRESS:

PHONE:

EMAIL:

BIRTHDAY:

>>>———<<<

NAME:

ADDRESS:

PHONE:

EMAIL:

BIRTHDAY:

>>>———<<<

NAME:

ADDRESS:

PHONE:

EMAIL:

BIRTHDAY:

NAME:

ADDRESS:

PHONE:

EMAIL:

BIRTHDAY:

>>>———<<<

NAME:

ADDRESS:

PHONE:

EMAIL:

BIRTHDAY:

>>>———<<<

NAME:

ADDRESS:

PHONE:

EMAIL:

BIRTHDAY:

NAME:

ADDRESS:

PHONE:

EMAIL:

BIRTHDAY:

>>———<<

NAME:

ADDRESS:

PHONE:

EMAIL:

BIRTHDAY:

>>———<<

NAME:

ADDRESS:

PHONE:

EMAIL:

BIRTHDAY:

NAME:

ADDRESS:

PHONE:

EMAIL:

BIRTHDAY:

>>>———<<<

NAME:

ADDRESS:

PHONE:

EMAIL:

BIRTHDAY:

>>>———<<<

NAME:

ADDRESS:

PHONE:

EMAIL:

BIRTHDAY:

J

NAME:

ADDRESS:

PHONE:

EMAIL:

BIRTHDAY:

>>>———<<<

NAME:

ADDRESS:

PHONE:

EMAIL:

BIRTHDAY:

>>>———<<<

NAME:

ADDRESS:

PHONE:

EMAIL:

BIRTHDAY:

J

NAME:

ADDRESS:

PHONE:

EMAIL:

BIRTHDAY:

>>>———<<<

NAME:

ADDRESS:

PHONE:

EMAIL:

BIRTHDAY:

>>>———<<<

NAME:

ADDRESS:

PHONE:

EMAIL:

BIRTHDAY:

J

NAME:

ADDRESS:

PHONE:

EMAIL:

BIRTHDAY:

>>>———<<<

NAME:

ADDRESS:

PHONE:

EMAIL:

BIRTHDAY:

>>>———<<<

NAME:

ADDRESS:

PHONE:

EMAIL:

BIRTHDAY:

J

NAME:

ADDRESS:

PHONE:

EMAIL:

BIRTHDAY:

>>> ———— <<<

NAME:

ADDRESS:

PHONE:

EMAIL:

BIRTHDAY:

>>> ———— <<<

NAME:

ADDRESS:

PHONE:

EMAIL:

BIRTHDAY:

K

NAME:

ADDRESS:

PHONE:

EMAIL:

BIRTHDAY:

>>>————<<<

NAME:

ADDRESS:

PHONE:

EMAIL:

BIRTHDAY:

>>>————<<<

NAME:

ADDRESS:

PHONE:

EMAIL:

BIRTHDAY:

K

NAME:

ADDRESS:

PHONE:

EMAIL:

BIRTHDAY:

NAME:

ADDRESS:

PHONE:

EMAIL:

BIRTHDAY:

NAME:

ADDRESS:

PHONE:

EMAIL:

BIRTHDAY:

K

NAME:

ADDRESS:

PHONE:

EMAIL:

BIRTHDAY:

NAME:

ADDRESS:

PHONE:

EMAIL:

BIRTHDAY:

NAME:

ADDRESS:

PHONE:

EMAIL:

BIRTHDAY:

K

NAME:

ADDRESS:

PHONE:

EMAIL:

BIRTHDAY:

>>> ———— <<<

NAME:

ADDRESS:

PHONE:

EMAIL:

BIRTHDAY:

>>> ———— <<<

NAME:

ADDRESS:

PHONE:

EMAIL:

BIRTHDAY:

L

NAME:

ADDRESS:

PHONE:

EMAIL:

BIRTHDAY:

>>—————<<

NAME:

ADDRESS:

PHONE:

EMAIL:

BIRTHDAY:

>>—————<<

NAME:

ADDRESS:

PHONE:

EMAIL:

BIRTHDAY:

L

NAME:

ADDRESS:

PHONE:

EMAIL:

BIRTHDAY:

>>>————<<<

NAME:

ADDRESS:

PHONE:

EMAIL:

BIRTHDAY:

>>>————<<<

NAME:

ADDRESS:

PHONE:

EMAIL:

BIRTHDAY:

L

NAME:

ADDRESS:

PHONE:

EMAIL:

BIRTHDAY:

>>———<<

NAME:

ADDRESS:

PHONE:

EMAIL:

BIRTHDAY:

>>———<<

NAME:

ADDRESS:

PHONE:

EMAIL:

BIRTHDAY:

L

NAME:

ADDRESS:

PHONE:

EMAIL:

BIRTHDAY:

>>>————<<<

NAME:

ADDRESS:

PHONE:

EMAIL:

BIRTHDAY:

>>>————<<<

NAME:

ADDRESS:

PHONE:

EMAIL:

BIRTHDAY:

M

NAME:

ADDRESS:

PHONE:

EMAIL:

BIRTHDAY:

>>>————<<<

NAME:

ADDRESS:

PHONE:

EMAIL:

BIRTHDAY:

>>>————<<<

NAME:

ADDRESS:

PHONE:

EMAIL:

BIRTHDAY:

M

NAME:

ADDRESS:

PHONE:

EMAIL:

BIRTHDAY:

NAME:

ADDRESS:

PHONE:

EMAIL:

BIRTHDAY:

NAME:

ADDRESS:

PHONE:

EMAIL:

BIRTHDAY:

NAME:

ADDRESS:

PHONE:

EMAIL:

BIRTHDAY:

NAME:

ADDRESS:

PHONE:

EMAIL:

BIRTHDAY:

NAME:

ADDRESS:

PHONE:

EMAIL:

BIRTHDAY:

M NAME:

ADDRESS:

PHONE:

EMAIL:

BIRTHDAY:

>>> ———— <<<

NAME:

ADDRESS:

PHONE:

EMAIL:

BIRTHDAY:

>>> ———— <<<

NAME:

ADDRESS:

PHONE:

EMAIL:

BIRTHDAY:

NAME:

ADDRESS:

PHONE:

EMAIL:

BIRTHDAY:

>>———<<

NAME:

ADDRESS:

PHONE:

EMAIL:

BIRTHDAY:

>>———<<

NAME:

ADDRESS:

PHONE:

EMAIL:

BIRTHDAY:

N NAME:

ADDRESS:

PHONE:

EMAIL:

BIRTHDAY:

>>>———<<<

NAME:

ADDRESS:

PHONE:

EMAIL:

BIRTHDAY:

>>>———<<<

NAME:

ADDRESS:

PHONE:

EMAIL:

BIRTHDAY:

NAME:

ADDRESS:

PHONE:

EMAIL:

BIRTHDAY:

>>>———<<<

NAME:

ADDRESS:

PHONE:

EMAIL:

BIRTHDAY:

>>>———<<<

NAME:

ADDRESS:

PHONE:

EMAIL:

BIRTHDAY:

N NAME:

ADDRESS:

PHONE:

EMAIL:

BIRTHDAY:

>>> ———— <<<

NAME:

ADDRESS:

PHONE:

EMAIL:

BIRTHDAY:

>>> ———— <<<

NAME:

ADDRESS:

PHONE:

EMAIL:

BIRTHDAY:

NAME:

ADDRESS:

PHONE:

EMAIL:

BIRTHDAY:

NAME:

ADDRESS:

PHONE:

EMAIL:

BIRTHDAY:

NAME:

ADDRESS:

PHONE:

EMAIL:

BIRTHDAY:

O NAME:

ADDRESS:

PHONE:

EMAIL:

BIRTHDAY:

>>>———<<<

NAME:

ADDRESS:

PHONE:

EMAIL:

BIRTHDAY:

>>>———<<<

NAME:

ADDRESS:

PHONE:

EMAIL:

BIRTHDAY:

O

NAME:

ADDRESS:

PHONE:

EMAIL:

BIRTHDAY:

>>———<<

NAME:

ADDRESS:

PHONE:

EMAIL:

BIRTHDAY:

>>———<<

NAME:

ADDRESS:

PHONE:

EMAIL:

BIRTHDAY:

O NAME:

ADDRESS:

PHONE:

EMAIL:

BIRTHDAY:

>>>———<<<

NAME:

ADDRESS:

PHONE:

EMAIL:

BIRTHDAY:

>>>———<<<

NAME:

ADDRESS:

PHONE:

EMAIL:

BIRTHDAY:

NAME: **P**

ADDRESS:

PHONE:

EMAIL:

BIRTHDAY:

>>>———<<<

NAME:

ADDRESS:

PHONE:

EMAIL:

BIRTHDAY:

>>>———<<<

NAME:

ADDRESS:

PHONE:

EMAIL:

BIRTHDAY:

P

NAME:

ADDRESS:

PHONE:

EMAIL:

BIRTHDAY:

>>> ———— <<<

NAME:

ADDRESS:

PHONE:

EMAIL:

BIRTHDAY:

>>> ———— <<<

NAME:

ADDRESS:

PHONE:

EMAIL:

BIRTHDAY:

P

NAME:

ADDRESS:

PHONE:

EMAIL:

BIRTHDAY:

>>>————<<<

NAME:

ADDRESS:

PHONE:

EMAIL:

BIRTHDAY:

>>>————<<<

NAME:

ADDRESS:

PHONE:

EMAIL:

BIRTHDAY:

P

NAME:

ADDRESS:

PHONE:

EMAIL:

BIRTHDAY:

>>> ———— <<<

NAME:

ADDRESS:

PHONE:

EMAIL:

BIRTHDAY:

>>> ———— <<<

NAME:

ADDRESS:

PHONE:

EMAIL:

BIRTHDAY:

Q

NAME:

ADDRESS:

PHONE:

EMAIL:

BIRTHDAY:

>>>————<<<

NAME:

ADDRESS:

PHONE:

EMAIL:

BIRTHDAY:

>>>————<<<

NAME:

ADDRESS:

PHONE:

EMAIL:

BIRTHDAY:

Q

NAME:

ADDRESS:

PHONE:

EMAIL:

BIRTHDAY:

>>>———<<<

NAME:

ADDRESS:

PHONE:

EMAIL:

BIRTHDAY:

>>>———<<<

NAME:

ADDRESS:

PHONE:

EMAIL:

BIRTHDAY:

Q

NAME:

ADDRESS:

PHONE:

EMAIL:

BIRTHDAY:

>>>———<<<

NAME:

ADDRESS:

PHONE:

EMAIL:

BIRTHDAY:

>>>———<<<

NAME:

ADDRESS:

PHONE:

EMAIL:

BIRTHDAY:

Q NAME:

ADDRESS:

PHONE:

EMAIL:

BIRTHDAY:

>>>———<<<

NAME:

ADDRESS:

PHONE:

EMAIL:

BIRTHDAY:

>>>———<<<

NAME:

ADDRESS:

PHONE:

EMAIL:

BIRTHDAY:

R

NAME:

ADDRESS:

PHONE:

EMAIL:

BIRTHDAY:

NAME:

ADDRESS:

PHONE:

EMAIL:

BIRTHDAY:

NAME:

ADDRESS:

PHONE:

EMAIL:

BIRTHDAY:

R NAME:

ADDRESS:

PHONE:

EMAIL:

BIRTHDAY:

>>> ———— <<<

NAME:

ADDRESS:

PHONE:

EMAIL:

BIRTHDAY:

>>> ———— <<<

NAME:

ADDRESS:

PHONE:

EMAIL:

BIRTHDAY:

R

NAME:

ADDRESS:

PHONE:

EMAIL:

BIRTHDAY:

NAME:

ADDRESS:

PHONE:

EMAIL:

BIRTHDAY:

NAME:

ADDRESS:

PHONE:

EMAIL:

BIRTHDAY:

R

NAME:

ADDRESS:

PHONE:

EMAIL:

BIRTHDAY:

>>> ———— <<<

NAME:

ADDRESS:

PHONE:

EMAIL:

BIRTHDAY:

>>> ———— <<<

NAME:

ADDRESS:

PHONE:

EMAIL:

BIRTHDAY:

S

NAME:
_____

ADDRESS:
_____
_____

PHONE:
_____

EMAIL:
_____

BIRTHDAY:
_____

>>> ——— <<<

NAME:
_____

ADDRESS:
_____
_____

PHONE:
_____

EMAIL:
_____

BIRTHDAY:
_____

>>> ——— <<<

NAME:
_____

ADDRESS:
_____
_____

PHONE:
_____

EMAIL:
_____

BIRTHDAY:
_____

S

NAME:

ADDRESS:

PHONE:

EMAIL:

BIRTHDAY:

>>> ———— <<<

NAME:

ADDRESS:

PHONE:

EMAIL:

BIRTHDAY:

>>> ———— <<<

NAME:

ADDRESS:

PHONE:

EMAIL:

BIRTHDAY:

S

NAME:

ADDRESS:

PHONE:

EMAIL:

BIRTHDAY:

>>> ———— <<<

NAME:

ADDRESS:

PHONE:

EMAIL:

BIRTHDAY:

>>> ———— <<<

NAME:

ADDRESS:

PHONE:

EMAIL:

BIRTHDAY:

S

NAME: _____

ADDRESS: _____

_____

PHONE: _____

EMAIL: _____

BIRTHDAY: _____

>>>———<<<

NAME: _____

ADDRESS: _____

_____

PHONE: _____

EMAIL: _____

BIRTHDAY: _____

>>>———<<<

NAME: _____

ADDRESS: _____

_____

PHONE: _____

EMAIL: _____

BIRTHDAY: _____

NAME:

ADDRESS:

PHONE:

EMAIL:

BIRTHDAY:

>>>———<<<

NAME:

ADDRESS:

PHONE:

EMAIL:

BIRTHDAY:

>>>———<<<

NAME:

ADDRESS:

PHONE:

EMAIL:

BIRTHDAY:

T NAME:

ADDRESS:

PHONE:

EMAIL:

BIRTHDAY:

>>>———<<<

NAME:

ADDRESS:

PHONE:

EMAIL:

BIRTHDAY:

>>>———<<<

NAME:

ADDRESS:

PHONE:

EMAIL:

BIRTHDAY:

T

NAME:

ADDRESS:

PHONE:

EMAIL:

BIRTHDAY:

>>>————<<<

NAME:

ADDRESS:

PHONE:

EMAIL:

BIRTHDAY:

>>>————<<<

NAME:

ADDRESS:

PHONE:

EMAIL:

BIRTHDAY:

T

NAME:

ADDRESS:

PHONE:

EMAIL:

BIRTHDAY:

>>>————<<<

NAME:

ADDRESS:

PHONE:

EMAIL:

BIRTHDAY:

>>>————<<<

NAME:

ADDRESS:

PHONE:

EMAIL:

BIRTHDAY:

U

NAME:

ADDRESS:

PHONE:

EMAIL:

BIRTHDAY:

>>> ———————— <<<

NAME:

ADDRESS:

PHONE:

EMAIL:

BIRTHDAY:

>>> ———————— <<<

NAME:

ADDRESS:

PHONE:

EMAIL:

BIRTHDAY:

U

NAME:

ADDRESS:

PHONE:

EMAIL:

BIRTHDAY:

>>> ———— <<<

NAME:

ADDRESS:

PHONE:

EMAIL:

BIRTHDAY:

>>> ———— <<<

NAME:

ADDRESS:

PHONE:

EMAIL:

BIRTHDAY:

U

NAME:

ADDRESS:

PHONE:

EMAIL:

BIRTHDAY:

>>>———<<<

NAME:

ADDRESS:

PHONE:

EMAIL:

BIRTHDAY:

>>>———<<<

NAME:

ADDRESS:

PHONE:

EMAIL:

BIRTHDAY:

U

NAME:

ADDRESS:

PHONE:

EMAIL:

BIRTHDAY:

>>>———<<<

NAME:

ADDRESS:

PHONE:

EMAIL:

BIRTHDAY:

>>>———<<<

NAME:

ADDRESS:

PHONE:

EMAIL:

BIRTHDAY:

V

NAME:

ADDRESS:

PHONE:

EMAIL:

BIRTHDAY:

>>>———<<<

NAME:

ADDRESS:

PHONE:

EMAIL:

BIRTHDAY:

>>>———<<<

NAME:

ADDRESS:

PHONE:

EMAIL:

BIRTHDAY:

V

NAME:

ADDRESS:

PHONE:

EMAIL:

BIRTHDAY:

>>>———<<<

NAME:

ADDRESS:

PHONE:

EMAIL:

BIRTHDAY:

>>>———<<<

NAME:

ADDRESS:

PHONE:

EMAIL:

BIRTHDAY:

V

NAME:

ADDRESS:

PHONE:

EMAIL:

BIRTHDAY:

NAME:

ADDRESS:

PHONE:

EMAIL:

BIRTHDAY:

NAME:

ADDRESS:

PHONE:

EMAIL:

BIRTHDAY:

V

NAME:

ADDRESS:

PHONE:

EMAIL:

BIRTHDAY:

>>>———<<<

NAME:

ADDRESS:

PHONE:

EMAIL:

BIRTHDAY:

>>>———<<<

NAME:

ADDRESS:

PHONE:

EMAIL:

BIRTHDAY:

NAME:

ADDRESS:

PHONE:

EMAIL:

BIRTHDAY:

>>>————<<<

NAME:

ADDRESS:

PHONE:

EMAIL:

BIRTHDAY:

>>>————<<<

NAME:

ADDRESS:

PHONE:

EMAIL:

BIRTHDAY:

W NAME: _____
ADDRESS: _____
_____
PHONE: _____
EMAIL: _____
BIRTHDAY: _____

>>>————<<<

NAME: _____
ADDRESS: _____
_____
PHONE: _____
EMAIL: _____
BIRTHDAY: _____

>>>————<<<

NAME: _____
ADDRESS: _____
_____
PHONE: _____
EMAIL: _____
BIRTHDAY: _____

W

NAME:

ADDRESS:

PHONE:

EMAIL:

BIRTHDAY:

>>>———<<<

NAME:

ADDRESS:

PHONE:

EMAIL:

BIRTHDAY:

>>>———<<<

NAME:

ADDRESS:

PHONE:

EMAIL:

BIRTHDAY:

W NAME:

ADDRESS:

PHONE:

EMAIL:

BIRTHDAY:

>>>———<<<

NAME:

ADDRESS:

PHONE:

EMAIL:

BIRTHDAY:

>>>———<<<

NAME:

ADDRESS:

PHONE:

EMAIL:

BIRTHDAY:

X

NAME:

ADDRESS:

PHONE:

EMAIL:

BIRTHDAY:

>>>————<<<

NAME:

ADDRESS:

PHONE:

EMAIL:

BIRTHDAY:

>>>————<<<

NAME:

ADDRESS:

PHONE:

EMAIL:

BIRTHDAY:

X

NAME:

ADDRESS:

PHONE:

EMAIL:

BIRTHDAY:

NAME:

ADDRESS:

PHONE:

EMAIL:

BIRTHDAY:

NAME:

ADDRESS:

PHONE:

EMAIL:

BIRTHDAY:

Y

NAME:

ADDRESS:

PHONE:

EMAIL:

BIRTHDAY:

>>> ———— <<<

NAME:

ADDRESS:

PHONE:

EMAIL:

BIRTHDAY:

>>> ———— <<<

NAME:

ADDRESS:

PHONE:

EMAIL:

BIRTHDAY:

Y

NAME:

ADDRESS:

PHONE:

EMAIL:

BIRTHDAY:

>>>————<<<

NAME:

ADDRESS:

PHONE:

EMAIL:

BIRTHDAY:

>>>————<<<

NAME:

ADDRESS:

PHONE:

EMAIL:

BIRTHDAY:

Y

NAME:

ADDRESS:

PHONE:

EMAIL:

BIRTHDAY:

>>>———<<<

NAME:

ADDRESS:

PHONE:

EMAIL:

BIRTHDAY:

>>>———<<<

NAME:

ADDRESS:

PHONE:

EMAIL:

BIRTHDAY:

Y

NAME:

ADDRESS:

PHONE:

EMAIL:

BIRTHDAY:

>>>————<<<

NAME:

ADDRESS:

PHONE:

EMAIL:

BIRTHDAY:

>>>————<<<

NAME:

ADDRESS:

PHONE:

EMAIL:

BIRTHDAY:

Z

NAME:

ADDRESS:

PHONE:

EMAIL:

BIRTHDAY:

>>>———<<<

NAME:

ADDRESS:

PHONE:

EMAIL:

BIRTHDAY:

>>>———<<<

NAME:

ADDRESS:

PHONE:

EMAIL:

BIRTHDAY:

Z

NAME:

ADDRESS:

PHONE:

EMAIL:

BIRTHDAY:

>>> ———— <<<

NAME:

ADDRESS:

PHONE:

EMAIL:

BIRTHDAY:

>>> ———— <<<

NAME:

ADDRESS:

PHONE:

EMAIL:

BIRTHDAY:

Printed in Great Britain
by Amazon